WRITTEN BY LINDA HAGER PACK
ILLUSTRATED BY PAT BANKS

Appalachian Toys *and* Games

FROM A TO Z

UNIVERSITY PRESS OF KENTUCKY

The story "Never Mind Them Watermelons" is used with permission of S. E. Schlosser and AmericanFolklore.net. All rights reserved.

THE UNIVERSITY PRESS OF KENTUCKY

Scholarly publisher for the Commonwealth, serving Bellarmine University, Berea College, Centre College of Kentucky, Eastern Kentucky University, The Filson Historical Society, Georgetown College, Kentucky Historical Society, Kentucky State University, Morehead State University, Murray State University, Northern Kentucky University, Transylvania University, University of Kentucky, University of Louisville, and Western Kentucky University. All rights reserved.

EDITORIAL AND SALES OFFICES

The University Press of Kentucky
663 South Limestone Street
Lexington, Kentucky 40508-4008
www.kentuckypress.com

17 16 15 14 13   5 4 3 2 1

Library of Congress Cataloging-in-Publication Data

Pack, Linda Hager.

Appalachian toys and games from a to z / Linda Hager Pack; illustrated by Pat Banks.

p. cm.

Includes bibliographical references.

ISBN 978-0-8131-4104-6 (hardcover : alk. paper) — ISBN 978-0-8131-4105-3 (epub) 1. Toys—Appalachian Region, Southern—Juvenile literature. 2. Games—Appalachian Region, Southern—Juvenile literature. I. Banks, Pat. II. Title.

GV1218.5.P34 2013
790.1'33—dc23
2012039759

Designed by Erin Bradley Dangar
www.dangardesign.com

Printed and bound in South Korea by PACOM KOREA Inc.

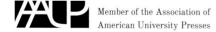 Member of the Association of American University Presses

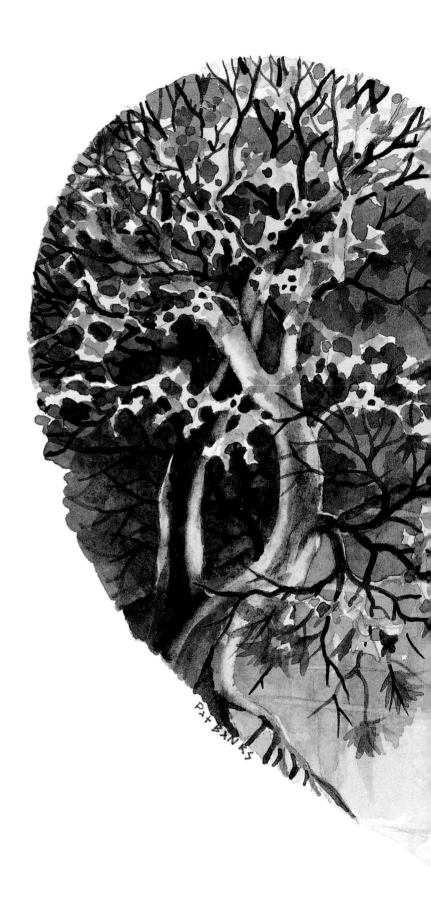

CONTENTS

THE BEGINNING

Join Appalachia's children for a rare glimpse into their lives of play during the mid to late 1800s. Explore the toys they enjoyed and the games they played during their growing-up years in the Appalachian Mountains.

Aa

IS FOR APPLE DOLL

Apple dolls have been made in the Appalachian Mountains for centuries. One gets the impression when looking at one of these dolls that it, too, has been around for centuries. And centuries. These wrinkled, wizened-looking dolls were fun to make because each carefully molded apple hid the secret of its personality until that "just right" moment when its furrowed brow and creased cheeks had dried long enough to release its special story. Would it be a man? Would it be a woman? Would it have the foot-stomping energy of a fiddle player, the soft eyes of a loving mother, the rustic face of a farmer, or the learned appearance of a schoolteacher?

The apple of choice for crafting an apple face was often the tart Rome Beauty. Apples used for doll making were picked in the fall, because apples picked earlier in the year were more prone to rot. Once the perfect apple was chosen to create a doll, most mountain women followed a similar procedure to create a one-of-a-kind face:

- *Peel a fresh apple but don't core it. Shave away any bruised spots.*

- *Make sure the stem of the apple is at the top of the head before beginning. Shape the facial features on the apple using a teaspoon. The tip of a butter knife can be used to outline the eyes, nose, and mouth.*

- *Soak the creation in salt water for about thirty-six hours. This helps to preserve the apple.*

- *Thread a string through the center of the apple. Hang the apple up in a dry, airy place and let it shrivel.*

It is up to the doll maker to decide what the doll's story is. And then to tell it.

Bb

IS FOR BUTTON ON A STRING, ALSO KNOWN AS BUZZ BUTTON

Easy to make and easy to work, the buzz button was often a child's toy of choice to pass away those rare moments of free time. Mountain people recycled and reused long before it became a slogan or a call-to-arms to take care of Mother Nature. All buttons were saved, and all children knew where those saved buttons were kept. A child needed only to take a button from the button box, get a piece of string about twice the length of her arm, thread the string crosswise through the button's eyes (the holes in the button), and tie the thread ends together, and a buzz button was born.

To work the toy, a child first had to wind the button tightly by spinning it forward on the string. A good technique was to position the button in the middle of the string, hold the string in place with the left hand, and spin it tightly with the right. Once the string was good and tight, the child pulled the string with both hands. And then released the pull. Pulled. Released. Pulled. Released. And the button would make a most marvelous buzzing sound. Hence the name buzz button.

Cc

IS FOR CORN SHUCK DOLL, ALSO KNOWN AS CORN HUSK DOLL

The earliest corn shuck dolls were crafted by Native Americans. That's because in order to make a doll out of corn husks, the doll maker had to have . . . corn! Corn originally grew only in the Americas, where scientists believe that native tribes living in the highlands of Mexico first cultivated the crop thousands of years ago. When the tribes from Mexico migrated north, they brought their corn with them. Corn later became the major crop for the Appalachians and is the number-one field crop in North America today.

It isn't clear whether the Native Americans taught their new Appalachian neighbors the tradition of making corn shuck dolls when they arrived in the mountains or whether the new settlers developed the skill independently. It is evident, however, that the Native Americans, the European settlers, and our African American ancestors all basically used the same technique to create these fragile fantasies of nature.

Corn shuck dolls were fairly simple to make.

The husks (the green outer wrappings on corn) were trimmed from the cob, dried in the sun from one to three days, and then soaked in warm water for about fifteen minutes. Four husks were laid one on top of another to form the doll's body, and a string was tied tightly around them about a thumb's length from the narrower end of the husks.

The tied end of the husks was turned upside-down and the loose husks were peeled downward like peeling a banana. The pulled-down husks were tied about an inch from the top to create a head. A fifth shuck was turned sideways, rolled up, and strings were tied around both ends for arms.

The arms were then slid up under a few of the loose body husks and held in place while another string was tied below the arms to form the waist of the doll. It was that simple.

Depending on the culture in which the doll was created, the doll might be adorned with a corn husk bonnet, apron, or broom, for example, or dressed with fabric clothing. The doll was not given a face. Perhaps the "Iroquois Legend of the Corn Husk Doll" will explain why.

THE IROQUOIS LEGEND OF THE CORN HUSK DOLL

The Iroquois people have what they call the three sisters, the "sustainers of life." These sisters are called corn, beans, and squash. The corn Spirit was so thrilled at being one of the sustainers of life that she asked the Creator what more she could do for her people. The Creator said that a beautiful doll could be formed from the husks.

The Creator set to work to form the doll. When finished, he gave the doll a beautiful face and sent it to the children of the Iroquois people to play with, and to make them happy.

The doll went from village to village, playing with the children and doing whatever she could for the children. Everywhere she went, everyone would tell her how beautiful she was, so after a while she became vain. The Creator spoke to her and explained that this was not the right kind of behavior, and she agreed not to be this way anymore. The Creator told her that if she continued with this behavior, he would punish her, but he would not tell her how he would do it. She agreed not to act that way again, and things went on as before.

One afternoon she was walking by a creek, and she glanced into the water. As she admired herself, she couldn't help thinking how beautiful she was, because indeed she was beautiful.

At this time the Creator sent a giant screech owl out of the sky, and it snatched her reflection from the water. When she looked again, she had no reflection. This was the punishment the Creator put upon her.

When an Iroquois mother makes a doll for her children, she tells them this legend. This is to remind the children that it is wrong to think they are better than anyone else, and they must know that the Creator has given a special gift to everyone.

This legend is taken from snowwowl.com.

Dd

IS FOR DROP THE HANDKERCHIEF

A tisket, a tasket, a green and yellow basket,
I sent a letter to my love, and on the way I dropped it.
A little child picked it up and put it in his pocket.

And it continues:

A little child picked it up and put it in his pocket,
his pocket, he put it in his pocket.

The words to this game flittered up hillsides, caught on treetops, and were carried off by breezes as mountain children sang out in schoolyards, churchyards, or anywhere there was enough space and enough young'uns to play this skipping-singing game. All that was needed was a hanky or any ol' cloth from the bag of rags that Mom was always a-savin'.

The rules of the game were easy to follow.

A child was chosen to be IT, she was given the handkerchief that was to be dropped during the game, and all of the other players formed a large circle.

The rules required that the children in the circle face the center while they sang the game's rhyme: "A tisket a tasket, a green and yellow basket." That way they had no way of knowing if IT dropped the hanky at their feet while she skipped her way around the outside of the circle. IT dropped the handkerchief behind a child standing in the circle! When the chosen child realized that the handkerchief had been dropped behind him, he picked it up and the chase was on!

Now this is where it got tricky. If the child with the handkerchief caught IT, then the child was safe and IT took another turn at dropping the handkerchief. If IT reached the empty space first, then IT was safe and the child with the hanky became IT and took a turn at dropping the handkerchief.

It has been said that even though skipping was required to play this game, boys often participated for two reasons: first, they got to run, and second, they got to chase girls.

Ee

IS FOR EERIE STORIES

Stories have always played an important role
in Appalachia's rich oral tradition. If there
was a story to tell, there was a child to sit at
the feet of the storyteller to listen. Especially
if the story was just the least bit scary. Or eerie.
Young faces anxiously held the gaze of the
storyteller as she pulled from her seemingly
endless trove of memorized tales about witches,
haints, and boogers. Some of her stories
entertained, some enlightened, and some
frightened her listeners beyond their wildest
hopes and dreams. No matter the story, it was
the theater of the master storyteller that kept
her audience at rapt attention: a whispered
word, a slight turn of the head, a narrowing of
the eyes, a tremor in the hand, an exaggerated
word here or there, a sudden movement toward
the audience, and then . . . You get the picture.

Each new telling of a tale was told with the
life of a brand new story, so listeners never
tired of hearing the same story repeated.
Especially if those listeners were children.
And . . . if the stories were eerie.

One such story was "Never Mind Them
Watermelons," as retold by S. E. Schlosser.

NEVER MIND THEM WATERMELONS

Well now, old Sam Gibb, he didn't believe in
ghosts. Not one bit. Everyone in town knew
the old log cabin back in the woods was
haunted, but Sam Gibb just laughed whenever
folks talked about it. Finally, the blacksmith
dared Sam Gibb to spend the night in the
haunted log cabin. If he stayed there until
dawn, the blacksmith would buy him a whole
cartload of watermelons. Sam was delighted.
Watermelon was Sam's absolute favorite
fruit. He accepted the dare at once, packed
some matches and his pipe, and went right
over to the log cabin to spend the night.

Sam went into the old log cabin, started a fire,
lit his pipe, and settled into a rickety old chair

with yesterday's newspaper. As he was reading, he heard a creaking sound. Looking up, he saw that a gnarled little creature with glowing red eyes had taken the seat beside him. It had a long, forked tail, two horns on its head, claws at the ends of its hands, and sharp teeth that poked right through its large lips.

"There ain't nobody here tonight except you and me," the creature said to old Sam Gibb. It had a voice like the hiss of flames. Sam's heart nearly stopped with fright. He leapt to his feet.

"There ain't going to be nobody here but you in a minute," Sam Gibb told the gnarled creature. He leapt straight for the nearest exit—which happened to be the window—and hi-tailed it down the lane lickety-split. He ran so fast he overtook two rabbits being chased by a coyote. But it wasn't long before he heard the pounding of little hooves, and the gnarled creature with the red eyes caught up with him.

"You're making pretty good speed for an old man," said the creature to old Sam Gibb.

"Oh, I can run much faster than this," Sam Gibb told it. He took off like a bolt of lightning, leaving the gnarled creature in the dust. As he ran passed the smithy, the blacksmith came flying out of the forge to see what was wrong.

"Never mind about them watermelons," Sam Gibb shouted to the blacksmith without breaking his stride.

Old Sam Gibb ran all the way home and hid under his bed for the rest of the night. After that, he was a firm believer in ghosts and spooks, and he refused to go anywhere near the old cabin in the woods.

This story was found on Americanfolklore.net and retold by S. E. Schlosser.

Ff

IS FOR FOX AND HOUNDS

There were times in the mountains when the sound of barking dogs chasing a lone fox could be heard for miles around and for hours at a time. If the listener paid close enough attention to what he was hearing, he would realize that the dogs were not of the four-legged variety. No, these dogs had only two legs, and they were relentless in chasing their prey. Deep into the forest they ran, struggling up hills, jumping creeks, climbing over rocks, ducking tree branches, and avoiding briar patches until they had treed their quarry. Once they found the fox, usually sitting high behind the leaves on a well-hidden branch, the hounds would bark and bark at the base of the tree to signal their catch.

It was easy to get caught up in a good game of Fox and Hounds. Once the fox was chosen, the game would begin. The fox was given a head start into the woods, where he would leave a hopefully deceiving trail of twigs for the hounds to follow. At some point the fox would break loose from his trail of twigs and travel as deep into the forest as he could get before hearing the hounds in hot pursuit. Once on their own, and without a trail to follow, the hounds communicated using their barks. Increased barking in a particular area meant the fox had been treed. It was a battle cry for all hounds to come running to where the poor fox, hidden in the branches of a tree, held on for dear life. The barking was a fearsome thing to hear—loud and aggressive—but the fox could do nothing but stay put until an agreement was reached for his capture. Then a new game could begin with a new fox.

When this game was played at school, the scholars sometimes got so carried away that a game they began at noon recess wouldn't bring them back to school until the school day was nearly over. We won't discuss what their teacher might have had to say about that! Or what happened on those rare occasions when a tree was chopped down to capture a truly sly fox.

Gg

IS FOR GAME OF GRACES

The Game of Graces is an old game that was probably best known in Virginia. It is believed that the game got its name because it encouraged gracefulness in movement. Even though the game was considered a good way to teach young ladies to be graceful, boys also enjoyed an occasional game with the sticks and hoop.

The Game of Graces required four dowels or sticks about eighteen inches long and a wooden hoop about nine inches across. The hoop was often wrapped in brightly colored ribbons. The ribbons made the hoop look pretty while sailing through the air, gave it a cushion, and make it easier to catch. It took two players to play Graces, and each player was given two dowels. The object of the game was to pass the hoop back and forth between the two players without dropping it. The first player would cross her sticks in the shape of an X, place the hoop over her sticks, and toss the hoop into the air to her opponent. The second player followed the trailing ribbons with her eyes and moved her body into position to catch the hoop. She could slide, step, skip, reach, stretch, and move in any direction; she could use both dowels or simply bring the hoop down with one. But when she was ready to throw the hoop back to her opponent, she first had to cross her sticks in an X, place the hoop on her sticks, and toss.

The game could be quite lovely to watch, especially if the participants were graceful.

Hh

IS FOR HOOP AND STICK

One guess what was needed to play this game. Yes! A hoop and a stick! Now . . . where did yesterday's children find a hoop? Normally the wooden hoop was taken from around a wooden barrel. Then the hunt was on to find a stick with the perfect bend for trundling the hoop along smooth surfaces and for controlling it when it needed to be still. After the necessary equipment was collected, the child was ready to follow the rules of the game:

- *Look for a good area on which to roll the hoop. (Dirt roads work well.)*

- *Roll the hoop with the bent stick.*

- *Run and roll, run and roll, run and roll, until you just can't run and roll any more.*

- *Game over. Or you may begin again.*

Children have been rolling and trundling hoops since the time of the ancient Egyptians. In 1000 BC, children in Egypt played with large hoops made out of dried grapevines. Artwork on ancient Greek vases shows hoops being used in play. Our colonists brought this simple game to North America from Europe, and in the late 1950s we began to use the popular hoop for something called the hula hoop. There are grandparents who have good memories of that fun hoop.

Ii

IS FOR IMAGINATION

With few toys and books in the home, Appalachia's children tapped into their deep wells of imagination to mine creative ways for solitary play. Making use of the resources they had on hand, many children went exploring in the mountains to gain entrance into childhood's magical world of make-believe. Girls and boys alike sought out clearings for playhouses, with privacy provided by the natural walls of trees, shrubs, and bushes. Large rocks were desirable for tables, beds, chairs, and shelves. Small stones were carefully laid on the ground to create additional rooms, form doorways, and produce walls that nature had failed to provide. Straw brooms were often made to keep a playhouse swept up nice and neat, moss was gathered to carpet the floor, and flowers were collected for decoration. Pieces of broken crockery were used to serve imagined dinners with queens and kings; sticks gathered from the forest floor were used as eating utensils; and cakes made from mud were presented with pride. When children wanted to add a touch of dress-up to their play, they gathered leaves, clover, flowers, grasses, twigs, and whatever else struck their fancy. Clover and grasses were often woven into jewelry, and leaf dresses were known to be quite stunning when held together with twigs. Especially in the fall.

Playhouses were private places; their locations were kept hush-hush. Some children preferred to build them near creeks, where they had easy access to smooth river rocks and driftwood; others preferred a place deep in the woods, where there were clusters of trees and boulders. Girls took dolls to their secret spots for hours of play. They were known to keep large sticks at strategic places so they could "clobber" any "rotten ol' boy" who happened to come by to mess things up. Boys especially didn't want anyone to know about their playhouses, which often hid their collections of gathered treasures.

Mountain children loved using their imaginations to create fantastic worlds of whimsy in which to play, just as children do today. The difference is . . . they had the whole outdoors in which to do it.

Jj

IS FOR JUMPING ROPE

Jumping rope was a favorite pastime in the mountains. All that was needed was something to use for a rope and several good jumping rhymes set to memory. Rope wasn't always available to Appalachia's children, so they made do. They gathered honeysuckle vine, tied rags together, occasionally used plough line, or attempted to turn any ol' piece of string they could save into a jump rope. They knew better than to borrow Daddy's rope from off the mules.

The game was normally associated with schoolgirls, but sometimes boys and girls who were nearly grown would join in the fun. It was played with two children holding the ends of a jump rope while a third child stood between them prepared to jump. A rhyme was sung and the actions were followed or the numbers counted until the jumper missed. Then it was someone else's turn to jump. Double Dutch was especially hard. The rope turners turned two ropes in opposite directions. At the same time! One can only imagine the difficulty of jumping "in" with two ropes turning simultaneously!

Jumping rope didn't originate in the mountains. Or even in the United States. Nor was it always a child's game. There is much research that can date rope jumping back to 1600 BC, when Egyptians used vines for jumping; there are researchers who also date it to ancient China. The Western version that we enjoy today probably began in Egypt, spread through Europe to the Netherlands, and finally made its way to North America by way of the Dutch settlers.

Jumping rope was usually accompanied by some type of singsong rhyme that either told a story or called out actions to follow. The following are a few examples of the many rhymes used for rope jumping:

CINDERELLA

Cinderella, dressed in yellow
Went upstairs to kiss her fellow
Made a mistake
And kissed a snake
How many doctors
Did it take?
1, 2, 3, 4, 5 . . .

DOWN IN THE VALLEY

This rhyme begins with the rope being swung back and forth instead of overhead. When the counting part begins, the rope is swung overhead.

Down in the valley
Where the green grass grows,
There sat Janey (insert jumper's name)
Sweet as a rose.
Along came Johnny
And kissed her on the cheek.
How many kisses
Did she get this week?
1, 2, 3, 4, 5 . . .

I LIKE COFFEE

The first jumper inserts the name of a friend she wants to join her in jumping. Then that friend inserts the name of another friend, who also joins them in jumping. The game continues until the group is too large to fit or until everyone is jumping.

I like coffee,
I like tea,
I'd like for Janey (insert jumper's name)
To come in with me.

Kk

IS FOR KICK THE CAN

Kick the Can was a fancied-up version of Hide and Seek. Except there was a can. And a jail. And, of course, a kicker. The first thing that had to be done to get up a good game of Kick the Can was to find a good clear area with lots of hiding places. Then there was the task of finding a can. But that wasn't too much of a problem, because tin cans had been present in the mountains since soldiers carried them in during the Civil War. Once the spot was found, the can was in hand, and the children had gathered, it was time to begin.

A spot for the can was marked as BASE and all players were made aware of it. A player was picked to be IT. A player who could kick well was chosen to be the KICKER. IT chose an area near BASE to be the JAIL.

Play began when the KICKER kicked the can as far away from BASE as he could get it. Everyone ran to find a hiding place while IT retrieved the can, put it down on BASE, closed his eyes, and counted slowly to ten.

The object then was for IT to spot the other players, call out their names, identify where they were hiding, and then beat them back to the CAN/BASE. Every player IT spotted and beat back to the CAN/BASE was placed in JAIL.

Players could be FREED from JAIL if another player beat IT to the CAN and kicked it as far into the distance as he could. When this happened, the jailbirds were released, and IT had to start all over: retrieving, counting to ten, and hunting.

The game continued until IT was able to get everyone in the JAIL or until all of the players were simply worn out from playing.

As you can see, this game had the potential to last a long time and to be fairly exhausting. Unless you found a really good hiding spot and the others forgot all about you!

Ll

IS FOR LIMBERJACK

The limberjack was a fascinating toy. It was a jointed wooden figure that danced, kicked its feet into the air, and twirled its arms up over its head. It looked like a puppet and acted like a dancing doll but worked like a foot-tapping, leg-slapping, hand-clapping rhythm instrument.

It was called by many names: slapjack, jiggerman, limberjim, limberjill, clog doll, dancin' dan, paddle puppet, and yankee-doodle dancer. The doll was held with its feet resting "just so" on the end of a bouncy board, waiting to spring into high-kicking action when the board was made to vibrate. The rhythmic tap-tap-tapping of the doll's wooden feet added to the excitement of any lively fiddle music. Plus it was a sight to watch the limberjack dance a jig on his own private bouncy stage!

To operate the limberjack, a child had to sit down and place one end of the bouncy board or paddle under her leg. She held onto the stick in the back of the limberjack, lowered him so his feet just barely touched the free end of the board, and then vibrated the board by gently bouncing it with her free hand. Wa! Lah! The limberjack was ready to be a toy or a rhythm instrument.

The limberjack had a long history in Europe before it made its way to the Appalachian Mountains, where it was given birth by the simple blade of a pocketknife. The English name "limberjack" came from the toy's loose, limber method of dancing and from the European name used for Everyman: Jack. Limberjack. The limberjack was, indeed, a fascinating toy!

Mm

IS FOR MARBLES

Marbles, sometimes known as marvils, was one of the most popular games enjoyed by early Appalachian children and men. The game was played in schoolyards, barnyards, and favorite dirt spots on the way home from school. Almost any mountain home that had children had a ring for playing Marbles. Friends often made arrangements to meet on Sundays after church for a friendly game of keepsies. They'd come with pouches and pockets filled to the brim with treasured globes of clay and glass. The bigger the marble collection, the better the skill of its owner.

There were three ways Appalachians could obtain marbles for playing: they could form them from available clay and then fire them in ashes shoveled from their own fireplaces; they could purchase glass marbles (usually made in West Virginia); or they could chip a small hole in a large rock and take out a small chunk of hard stone called "marvel rock" (not real marble but the hardest rock that could be found in the mountains), then place the chunk in a creek so that the running water forced the stone to turn over and over until it was round.

Once a game began, the air was charged with the laughter of children and the clinking sound of taws (larger, shooting marbles) being shot into circles of coveted marbles. Some players carried little pads or pieces of fur on which to rest their knuckles, but that still didn't prevent bruising as a result of long hours of marble contests. After the last marble was shot out of the ring, all of the winnings had been pocketed, and the sun was setting low in the sky, the players headed home.

There were steps that had to be followed when getting ready to play Marbles, rules that had to be obeyed, and a vocabulary that had to be learned.

HOW MARBLES WAS PLAYED

The first thing that had to be decided in a game of Marbles was whether the game was going to be a game of friendlies or a game of keepsies. All players were allowed to keep the marbles they brought in a game of friendlies. Not so in a game of keepsies. Players went home with their winnings after a game of keepsies.

Next the players chose a game. Let's choose probably the most popular game, Bull Ring or Ringer. This game required only a large circle to be drawn in the dirt, usually about eight feet in diameter, and an agreed-upon number of marbles to be placed in the middle by each player.

The players determined who shot first by "laggin' for the line." A line was drawn in the dirt, and each player rolled or flipped a marble toward the line. The person whose marble got the closest to the line played first.

Each player chose his taw and placed his playing marbles in the middle of the ring, and the player who had won the lag began the play.

A player was allowed to continue play as long as he knocked marbles out of the ring (without touching another marble) and his taw remained inside the ring.

Each time a player took a new turn, he shot from where his taw had previously landed.

A player forfeited his turn when he failed to knock a marble out, when he touched another marble in the ring, or when his taw rolled outside the ring.

Play continued until all of the marbles were knocked out of the ring and claimed; until the recess bell rang, calling the players to return to class; or until the sun went down and the players could no longer see.

Nn

IS FOR NOISEMAKERS

Mountain children (and adults) had a rip-roaring good time playing with toys that roared, swished, clattered, jingled, whistled, hummed, banged, whizzed, buzzed, and just made a racket in general. All that was usually needed to create such an ear-teasing noise was a good pocketknife, an occasional length of string, and a trip into the woods. Even the names of these toys sounded interesting as they rolled off the tongue: dumb bull, bull roarer, whizzer, flipperdinger, cornstalk fiddle, whistle, buzz button, buzz saw, and crow call.

One of the easiest noisemakers to make was the bull roarer. This toy consisted of three parts: a thin paddle whittled down to about 10 inches long by 3 inches wide, a 10-inch handle or sturdy stick (rhododendron worked best), and about 3 to 5 feet of strong waxed string to attach the two together. Once completed, the bull roarer could be swung over the head in a circular motion or in the shape of an X.

You might guess that Appalachians gave this toy its name because some thought it sounded a bit like an angry bull a-bellerin'. What you might not guess is that the bull roarer isn't unique to the southern Appalachian Mountains. It has existed for many thousands of years in other time periods, in other cultures, and on other continents. If you visit Europe, Asia, or Africa, you might spot one on your journey.

Oo

IS FOR OUTSIDE

Outside is where June bugs flew
at the ends of strings,
Worms dangled from fishing lines,
And lightning bugs flickered
on warm summer evenings.

Outside is where the phases
of the moon were studied,
First stars of the evening were wished upon,
And daydreams wrapped themselves
around white clouds.

Outside is where forest treasures were pocketed,
Trees were climbed,
And necklaces of clover were braided.

Outside is where toes were dipped,
Rocks were skipped,
And laughing children dropped from ropes
at favorite water holes.

Outside is where honeysuckle was tasted,
Grapevines swung on,
And skipping games played.

Outside is where snipes were hunted,
Races run,
And wagons pulled.

Outside is where crawdads were caught,
Blackberries picked,
And terrapins investigated.

Outside is where music was played
on front porches,
Stories were told by kerosene lamps,
And dolls were rocked on stone steps.

Outside is where ropes were tugged in war,
Children were hid and sought,
And horseshoes ringed iron posts.

Outside is where snowballs were aimed,
Sleds raced downhill,
And sock-layered feet glided on ice.

Outside is where a child went to be a child.

Pp

IS FOR PICK-UP-STICKS OR JACKSTRAWS

One, two, buckle my shoe.
Three, four, shut the door.
Five, six, pick up sticks.

We are all familiar with this old nursery rhyme. But did you realize that it included the game of Pick-up-Sticks? Or that the game has been in the United States since our young country was only thirteen colonies?

The game has been called Selahtikàn by Native Americans, Spellicans by the British, Spilikins by the Canadians, Jerk-Straws by many Europeans, Jackstraws by the Hawaiians, and Pick-up-Sticks and Jackstraws by people in the United States. The origin of Pick-up-Sticks is unclear. Some believe that its roots lie deep in the Native American culture, where the game was played with straws of wheat. Others believe that the game of Spellicans originated in ancient China, where sticks of familiar shapes (spears, saws, snakes on a staff, etc.) were first made out of ivory. What is certain is that this game made its way into the Appalachian Mountains and into the hands of its young'uns.

The game of Pick-up-Sticks, as we know it today, developed from straws of wheat and splinters into the thin, straw-shaped pieces of wood that we are familiar with. There was usually a black helper stick and twenty-four brightly colored playing sticks. The playing sticks came in six colors and were assigned point values according to those colors.

To begin play, the bundle of playing sticks was held about a stick's height above the table and released haphazardly into a pile. The person releasing the sticks took the first turn at attempting to remove one stick at a time without causing any of the other sticks to move. This had to be done with one's hands unless the player was fortunate enough to

remove the black stick, which she was allowed to use as a helper. A player's turn continued as long as she was able to remove sticks without disturbing any of their neighbors. Each player got to keep every stick she was able to remove successfully. Play moved to the left, and the person with the most points at the end of the game (after all of the sticks had been picked up) was the winner.

The game of Jackstraws was perhaps a forerunner of Pick-up-Sticks in some mountain communities. Like the ancient Chinese Spellicans, the Appalachian Jackstraws were familiar hand-carved replicas of tools and utensils. Included in the different designs were likely to be mallets, hatchets, spades, anvils, shovels, saws, rakes, gourd dippers, and so forth. There was little difference between Pick-up-Sticks and the Jackstraws played in the mountains. A peg with a bent nail hooked in its end took the place of the black helping stick, and points were normally assigned to the jackstraws according to the difficulty involved in removing them from a pile.

You'll have to agree that picking up miniature mountain tools and utensils would be much more fun than just picking up straws and splinters.

Qq

IS FOR QUIET GAMES

When weather kept families inside their homes or scholars inside their school, children were required to play quiet games. Sometimes they would bring out homemade toys such as dolls, spinning tops, Jacob's ladders, puzzles, and carved animals. Other times they would engage in games such as Bum, Bum, Bum (charades), Pleased and Displeased, blindfold games, and Button, Button, Who's Got the Button?

The mother in the family usually had a box of buttons tucked safely away somewhere in the house. If a piece of clothing was outgrown or worn out and needed to be recycled into something different, say, a quilt, then any buttons on the clothing were snipped off and saved for future use. One of those uses, if a child could get her hands on the button box, was to play Button, Button, Who's Got the Button?

Once the ideal button was selected from the button box, a child was chosen to be IT, and the rest of the players sat in a circle with their palms together, thumbs up, in front of their chests. There was no limit to the number of children who could play.

IT placed the button inside her closed palms and moved around the entire circle carefully swiping her hands between the slightly opened palms of the other players. Without letting anyone know what she was doing, she carefully dropped the button into the closed palms of one of the players.

After IT made her full circle, the players called out, "Button, button, who's got the button?" IT called on three people to guess who had the button. If one of the players guessed correctly, he got to be IT. If none of the three chosen

players guessed who had the button, the child who held the button got to be IT and took a turn passing around the button.

Buttons have played an important role in man's artistic and decorative history. King Francis I ruled in France during the sixteenth century, where man's first appreciation for the artistry and beauty of buttons was born. The king's infatuation with buttons once prompted him to have a formal costume adorned with 13,600 shiny ornate buttons.

Rest assured that our Appalachian ancestors did not adorn themselves with buttons that were handmade, hand-painted works of art. They did, however, know how to have fun with simple wooden ones.

Rr

IS FOR RAG DOLLS

A little girl's rag doll was carried, snuggled, rocked, and loved throughout an entire childhood. Toys were scarce in the mountains, and making a rag doll from scraps of fabric was one way an Appalachian mother could grant her daughter's wish for a doll. Rag dolls were soft and huggable, and the materials needed to create them could usually be found in the home.

Fabric was at a premium in the mountains and was used primarily to sew clothing; even fabric from flour and feed sacks was put to good use. Any material left over from making clothing was used to cut quilt pieces. So only the smallest scraps of fabric that fell away from sewing projects were available to make the much-loved, much-played-with, aptly named rag dolls.

So how were these handmade fabric wonders created? Normally the dolls weren't sewn, but rather scraps of material were rolled together and then tied to form legs, arms, and a body. Children learned how to fashion these primitive dolls themselves and would often design an entire rag doll family. It is never too late to be introduced to a rag doll. It is an introduction well worth making.

Ss

IS FOR SLINGSHOT

There were three things most self-respecting mountain boys usually had in their possession: a Russell Barlow knife, a pocketful of marbles, and a slingshot. A slingshot was sometimes considered a toy and sometimes considered a hunting weapon. It could be used for shooting rocks at targets, or, if a boy was really good with a slingshot, it could be used to hunt small animals for food. Some boys carried their slingshots in their pockets and some hung them around their necks; but no matter where a boy kept his slingshot, it was always at the ready.

A boy had to invest a considerable amount of time to collect the necessary materials to make a slingshot. First he would make a trip into the woods to find a perfect Y-shaped forked branch for the body of the slingshot; usually a branch from a dogwood tree was the wood of choice. Then he could only hope to find some rubber from a red inner tube; a black inner tube wasn't as desirable because it lacked the elasticity of the red. Lastly, he was on the lookout for a good piece of leather (and yes, it had to be leather) to use for the shot pocket. Fortunately for our mountain boy, the tongue of an old shoe usually worked just fine.

When it came to actually shooting the slingshot, some skill was involved. A shoot was better when it was made with the body at a right angle to the target, feet apart, and weight balanced on both feet. It was the hand up front that actually controlled the slingshot rather than the hand that was releasing the stone. These skills were learned quickly, and the slingshot was used wisely. Most of the time.

Tt

IS FOR TOM WALKERS

Tom Walkers were actually gifts given to children by Mother Nature herself. The trick to owning a pair of these prized "walkin' crutches" or "stilts" was having a good eye for forked tree limbs or saplings while trekking through the woods. Naturally, the Tom Walkers worked best if the two forked limbs were shaped alike and the fork was cut at about the same distance from the ground.

The object of playing with Tom Walkers was to place one's feet in the forks and walk as far or as fast as one could walk—on the road, in the fields, across the creek. Most children began walking on beginner stilts, forked just a few inches off the ground. Some were able to graduate to taller stilts with forks that might be two feet tall or taller. Once a child's feet were situated in the forks, he would guide the Tom Walkers by holding them in his hands and lifting them up and down. This helped him to increase his pace and steady himself. But nothing could prevent the wear-and-tear the forks caused on a good pair of leather shoes.

If a child was really good on Tom Walkers, he could wade a creek without getting his feet wet. Now that is saying something!

Uu

IS FOR UMPIRE

Games involving a round ball can be simple or complex. The ones that are complex are usually better played and enjoyed when an umpire is in command. The umpire's job is to keep the game honest and make sure that all rules are followed. Such was the case when Appalachia's children brought their homemade twine and yarn balls to challenge opponents in pastures and schoolyards.

One game, Townball, needed three bases, a home plate, a pitcher, a catcher, and up to two dozen fielders on each side. The game was easy enough to play, and every player on a team got to bat when it was his team's turn at the plate. The batter sat down only when someone caught his ball (in the air or on the first bounce) or when he was thrown out at a base. This is how it worked:

Two teams were chosen.

To determine which team got to bat first, the bat was thrown into the air by one team captain and caught by the opposing team captain; then the captains took turns stacking their hands up the bat until one reached the top. The team of the captain who came closest to the top, without going over, got to bat first.

The fielding team had a pitcher and a catcher, and that was it. The bases were marked, but no one played a base. The players all played in the field.

A batter was called "out" if someone caught his fly ball in the air or on its first bounce. A runner was called "out" if the ball was thrown between him and the base he was running toward. Nothing was out-of-bounds. Another version of the game required the runner to be struck by the ball to be called out. Ouch!

One team batted until every player had been caught out; then the opposing team took a turn at bat.

And so the game continued. Each time a team scored, it received a tally. The game was over when one team reached the predetermined number of tallies (sometimes one hundred), or the game might be played for the number of innings that had been previously decided.

Does this game sound a little familiar?

V v

IS FOR VAULTING AND SWINGING

Trees provided a great deal of fun in the Appalachian Mountains. Children pumped their feet from handmade rope swings— viewing the world over bare toes and sunlit leaves. Swaying back and forth, mountain children enjoyed being suspended in a rhythmic flight of imagination high above the ground. Swinging was a fairly safe endeavor to enjoy with a tree. Vaulting, however, was only for the brave and daring.

Vaulting involved climbing up to the very top of a tall tree, crawling out to the end of a smaller, bendy branch, and then riding it over to the top branch of another tree. And hanging on for dear life, of course! Sound scary? You bet it was! Mountain boys could make their way down a steep mountain slope without a foot ever touching ground. As scary as that sounds, there was an even scarier way to vault in a tree.

Sometimes several boys would climb up to one of the tallest branches in a tree and ride it all the way down to the ground. Then . . . then all the boys but one would get off the branch and leave that one boy to ride the branch all the way back up to the top of the tree. Like a slingshot! Can you even imagine? This is one of those things that you DO NOT want to try at home.

Ww

IS FOR WHIMMYDIDDLE, OR GEE-HAW WHIMMYDIDDLE, AS IT IS ALSO KNOWN

The whimmydiddle was an intriguing toy that boys fashioned using their trusted pocketknives and sticks gathered from the forest. This toy was known by several different names. It was called a hoodoo stick by the Cherokee, a ziggerboo by some in Tennessee, a geehaw in Georgia, and a lie detector by many in Ohio. The toy consisted of two parts: a notched stick with a spinner or whirligig on the end and a smaller rubbing stick. Many boys preferred to use ivy branches to create their whimmydiddles because ivy had a natural curve to it that made the toy easier to hold.

The trick to playing with a whimmydiddle was knowing how to make the toy respond to the verbal commands of "gee" and "haw." When the operator of the toy said "gee," the toy would spin to the right. When he said "haw," the toy would spin to the left. How, one wonders, did he do that? It all had to do with the placement of his fingers on the notched stick. To make the propeller turn right, the boy would hold his index finger (the pointer finger) on the rubbing stick so that its tip would slide along the far side of the notches.

To make the whirligig turn to the left, the boy would rub the stick so that the thumb holding the rubbing stick would rub against the notched stick.

The "gee" and "haw" of this toy have a history that is good to know in order to understand the mysterious workings of its verbal commands. Gee and haw were traditionally and universally used with cattle and horses. Gee was the command given to make the horses, oxen, or cattle turn right. Haw was the command given to make the animals turn left.

Can you believe that these commands are believed to be the same all over the world?

Xx

IS FOR X MARKS THE SPOT, AS IN HOPSCOTCH

Hopscotch was a hopping game, as its name implies. Little was needed to start a rousing game of Hopscotch in the Appalachian Mountains: a level dirt playing area, a good stick with which to draw the playing court, some stones to use for markers, and a few friends with whom to play. Perfect.

Now the basics of the game:

First, line off a dirt hopscotch court using a stick: 1 single square, 2 side-by-side squares, 1 single square, 2 side-by-side squares, 1 single square, and 1 circle at the end for a resting spot.

Number the squares 1 to 9.

The first player tosses her marker into the #1 square. She hops on one foot over that square into square #2. She continues through the hopscotch court using one foot in the single squares and two feet in the side-by-side squares (one foot in each) until she reaches the end of the court. She is allowed to put both feet on the ground and rest while in the end circle preparing for her return.

When the player reaches the #2 square on returning, she picks up her marker and hops over #1 to the outside of the court. She must not skip any square (other than the one with her marker), step on any lines, touch the ground with her hands, or put both feet down in a hop square.

If the player is successful, she gets another turn and begins by tossing her marker into the #2 square, and so forth.

If the player commits an error, her marker is left where it is, and her turn is over. She will begin in that same square at her next turn.

The first player to make her way through all of the squares and back is the winner.

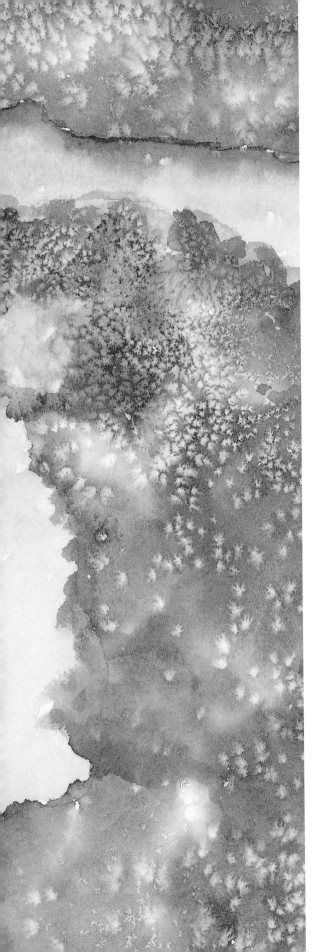

Yy

IS FOR YARD GAMES

There were many games that were played outdoors in mountain yards: Horseshoes, Hide-and-seek, Red Rover, Marbles, Mumbley Peg, foot races, relays, and Farmer-in-the-Dell, to name just a few. One of the most favorite yard games, hands down, was Anty Over. It required a ball (frequently made out of yarn), a building (usually the school), and two teams of players. The object of the game was to capture players from the opposing team while protecting all the players on your own team.

This is how it was played: A rhyme was said or a discussion held to determine which team got possession of the ball. The two teams took their positions on opposite sides of the school.

"Anty Over!" echoed through the trees, and the game was set in motion. The team with the ball, Team A, chose a powerful player to throw the ball over the building.

If a player on the opposing team, Team B, caught the ball, the battle was on! Team A's mission was to run to the other side of the building, where its players would be considered safe and off-limits to Team B. Team B's mission was to "tag out" Team A's players with the ball before they could reach the safety of the Team B side. This could be done in one of two ways: (1) The child who caught the ball could throw the ball at a player on the opposing team and tag him out, or (2) the child who caught the ball could hold on to the ball and pass it around to other players on his team, thus allowing fellow teammates the opportunity to tag out players on the opposing team.

Once a child had been tagged out, that child had to join the rival team. Sometimes the team with the ball would try to trick the other team by having all of its players run around the building with their hands behind their backs as if each player had the ball in his possession.

If Team B failed to catch the ball when it was thrown over the building, it forfeited the opportunity to catch members of Team A and had to put the ball back in play by shouting "Anty over" and throwing the ball back to Team A.

The game continued until all team members from one team had been captured. Then, of course, new teams could be chosen and the game could begin anew. And continue until the recess bell rang, until it was time for dinner, until the sun went down, or until the players' legs gave out.

Zz

IS FOR PUZZLES

Some of the most fun Appalachian children and adults had was engaging in the head-scratching, thought-provoking, time-consuming art of working puZZles!

Discarded nails, used horseshoes, intricately notched and fitted pieces of wood, and sections of carefully linked chains could all be ingeniously carved, bent, bowed, formed, and fastened with nary a dollop of glue, screw, or heat of fire to entertain for hours on end. All it took was a sharp mind, good eyes, and quick hands.

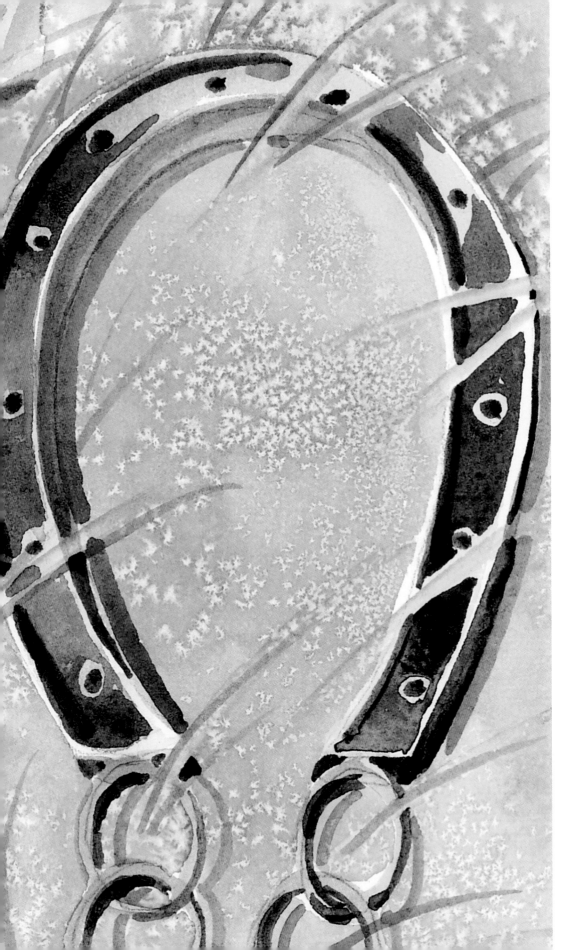

GLOSSARY

BOOGER
A goblin.

HAINT
A ghost.

MUMBLEY PEG
Mumbley Peg is played with a pocketknife. A circle is drawn in the dirt. The players take turns flipping their knives off their arms into the circle in the dirt. The player who makes his knife stick inside the circle the most times is the winner.

PLEASED AND DISPLEASED
This is an inside game. The players sit in a circle. Each player takes a turn acting as interrogator. The interrogator asks the player whose turn it is, "Are you pleased or displeased?" If the player is pleased, then the question moves to the next player. If the next player is displeased, the question is asked, "What would it take to please you?" The player states what it would take to please him, and whatever he says must be done. (Example: "It would please me for Jim to stand in the middle of the circle and dance the flat foot while Tom hums 'She'll Be Coming Round the Mountain.'")

SCHOLAR
A student.

SNIPE
A snipe was an imaginary animal. Boys would ask someone new to the mountains, or a younger boy, to go on a snipe hunt with them, and then they would sneak off and leave their guest to hunt by himself for sometimes hours before he caught on that he was all alone.

TRUNDLING
To trundle a hoop means to roll a hoop.

AUTHOR'S NOTE

Childhood has always beckoned me. I had no sooner stepped beyond its borders than it flirted with me to come back. "Come play," it whispered. So I became a teacher. I immersed myself in the world of children's literature. And I began to write for children.

Appalachia is my home. My people. I have been on a forty-year journey to gain a better understanding of and appreciation for the rich mountain heritage that sets the Appalachian apart. It is a heritage steeped with tradition, ripe with stories, alive with music, colored with an antique language, and born of the sweat and courage of those who came before.

Whenever I opened a book on my journey to "Appalachia enlightenment," whenever I visited a museum, hiked in the mountains, took a class, or spoke with a ranger in the Great Smoky Mountains National Park, it was always the children of long ago that I carried with me. It was their voices I heard, their play I envisioned, their toys I sought out, and their education I thirsted to know more about. The more I learned about how hard the children worked to help feed and care for the mountain family, the more interested I became in how they chose to spend those rare moments when they were free to play.

The decision to write this book was an easy one; the time period in which to place it took considerably more thought. Time had a way of keeping its own counsel in the mountains. It mattered little when Levi Strauss created his wonderful jeans, when the sewing machine was first built, when buttons first appeared on clothing, when seed and flour began to be sold in printed fabric sacks, or when the tin can was invented. What mattered was when these things made their way into the mountains. After careful consideration I decided to place the book in the mid to late 1800s. I was able to read interviews with people who had actually lived during that time; it took the mountain people beyond the Civil War; and by that time, after the Civil War, tin cans had made their way into the mountains.

I grew up in West Virginia, the only state entirely within the Appalachian Mountain range. Like my father before me and his father before him, I played many of the games that are included in this book. Except for one game, my father played all the games that I have written about. It is my hope that this book will spark a warm memory in the hearts of those who have played these old games and set off fireworks of curiosity for the new generation of children who have not.

As always, I hope that Appalachia's children will read this book and come away with a pride for who they were, who they are, and who they will always be.

ILLUSTRATOR'S NOTE

Linda Pack asked me to share my creative process with our readers to help them understand how an idea becomes an illustration.

The story you want to tell visually should support and enhance the text. I visualize what is happening or what is being described on the page. I research the subject matter and work with the author. I might take a field trip, draw from my own experiences, and sketch and photograph reference materials. Then I think about the way I want the images to flow on the page. I think about what perspective I want to use. Will I take a bird's-eye view, or will it be a panoramic view, or will I choose a close, intimate perspective?

After all of that "thinking" and researching, I am ready to sketch. I generally map out the pages in cartoon form. These are rough sketches; they help me think about the whole book at once. For me it is important to have the "big" picture before I start working on the details. When I am satisfied with the direction of my work, I will start sketching onto watercolor paper. I will work on three or four paintings at the same time and develop the values, textures, and depth of color that emphasize the idea on the page and further inform the viewer.

PLACES TO VISIT

Want to know more about Appalachia? Visit these places:

GEORGIA

MOUNTAIN CITY
Foxfire Museum and Heritage Center

KENTUCKY

WHITESBURG
Appalshop Community Arts & Media Center

MIDDLESBORO
Coal House Museum

HARLAN
Festival of the Mountain Masters

BENHAM
Kentucky Coal Mining Museum

PAINTSVILLE
Mountain Homeplace Living Museum

VAN LEAR
Van Lear Historical Society
    Coal Camp Museum

NORTH CAROLINA

CHEROKEE
Cherokee Heritage Museum
Oconaluftee Indian Village
Oconaluftee Farmstead
Great Smoky Mountains National Park

BOONE
Hickory Ridge Homestead &
    Living History Museum

BRASSTOWN
John C. Campbell Folk School

CULLOWHEE
North Carolina's Mountain Heritage Center
Western Carolina University

KENLY
Tobacco Farm Life Museum

OHIO

DAYTON
Mountain Days Festival

TENNESSEE

GREAT SMOKY MOUNTAINS NATIONAL PARK
Little Greenbrier School
Cades Cove

CUMBERLAND GAP
Cumberland Gap National Historical Park

SOUTHSIDE
Historic Collinsville

ATHENS
McMinn County Living Heritage Museum

NORRIS
Museum of Appalachia

GATLINBURG
Roaring Fork Motor Trail
Bud Ogle home

VONORE
Sequoyah Birthplace Museum

VIRGINIA

STAUNTON
Frontier Culture Museum
(aka Museum of American Frontier Culture)

GATE CITY
Homeplace Mountain Farm and Museum

WEST VIRGINIA

BECKLEY
Beckley Exhibition Coal
Youth Museum of Southern West
    Virginia & Mountain Homestead

HUNTINGTON
Heritage Farm Museum and Village

ACKNOWLEDGMENTS

It is with warmest appreciation that I acknowledge the following:

LAURA SUTTON
Laura was my editor and Christmas Angel at the University Press of Kentucky. She is the person who went to bat for Pat and me at University Press of Kentucky and promoted our first book there. Thank you, Laura, for everything I know you have done and the many things of which I am unaware. I miss you terribly!

THE UNIVERSITY PRESS OF KENTUCKY
Thank you, dear people, for allowing me the opportunity to share our rich Appalachian heritage with Appalachia's children. And beyond. It is an honor to be a member of your publishing family. A special thank you to Ashley Runyon for her good care of this book and to Lois Crum for her careful editing.

BEVERLY AND SHIRLEY DEZARN
They opened their hearts and the Bend School to us for an entire day so the children in this book could play with traditional folk toys and participate in old Appalachian games. Several years ago Beverly and Shirley spent a great deal of time and elbow grease lovingly bringing the Bend School back to life. We sincerely appreciate the additional time they spent readying the school for our visit.

Beverly and Shirley participated in our "Appalachian Yesterday," and Mr. D taught the children how to play Anty Over, Townball, and Marbles. These lovely people were gracious, knowledgeable, welcoming, and great fun! Mr. D shared a wealth of information with me about his personal experiences of growing up attending a one-room school (Bend School) and playing the old games that are shared in this book. Thanks to Beverly and Shirley, our book has the realistic background of a school built in the mid-1800s. Thank you, Beverly and Shirley.

THE CHILDREN
We would like to thank the following children for giving up a summer day to participate in an Appalachian Experience at Bend School. These children were cheerful, patient, and always agreeable to do anything the illustrator and I asked them to do to get an authentic "feel" for a particular game or toy. They also were gracious, friendly, and great fun! We are proud they agreed to be part of this book. Their names are:

JOHN BABUKA	LOGAN MIDDLETON
KAILEY BOYER	NICK MIDDLETON
KINSEY BOYER	MATTHEW NASSIDA
LAUREN CLOSS	JAMIE ORR
JESSICA COTTRELL	KAMERON PRESNELL
JORDON COTTRELL	BRIANNA RICHISON
PAGE GABBARD	LEAH THOMAS
ELLEIGH MCDANIEL	

THE PARENTS AND GRANDPARENTS
I will always treasure the day I spent with the outstanding children who selflessly donated their time so that photographs could be taken to illustrate Appalachian Toys and Games from A to Z. I thank their parents and grandparents for allowing them to participate in this book, for taking the time to prepare their clothing, for sharing photographs with Pat and me, and for all of the glorious help they gave me to get set up and to pack things away after the photo shoot. You are "stars" in my book!

THE PHOTOGRAPHERS
Kudos to the wonderful "parent photographers" who added their beautiful photographs to the ones Pat Banks and I took at Bend School. It has been a blessing to be able to see the children through the eyes of their loving parents. The photographers' names are:

JANE ANDERSON	ROBIN MCDANIEL
SHONDA BOYER	TAMMY RICHISON

JIM PACK, MY HUSBAND
Thank you for the support given, the words spoken, and the confidence shared that always give me that "needed boost."

BOB HAGER, MY DAD
Thank you for sharing the experiences you had while playing these games as a young boy. I love you, Dad.

ROBIN MCDANIEL, MY DAUGHTER
Thank you for your contribution to our day at Bend School. And for growing up to be my dearest friend.

JOSH PACK, MY SON
Thank you for always supporting my writing and for all the times you edited my work. Love you!

MERLE ROSE
Merle has been a good friend since we were in our early twenties. I tell him that he can do anything, and it is the truth! A huge "thank you" to Merle for making the authentic Tom Walkers and the bat we used for Townball.

S. E. SCHLOSSER
S. E. Schlosser retold "Never Mind Them Watermelons" from the state of Alabama on Americanfolklore.net. Thank you, Mr. Schlosser, for giving us permission to use your story. It is a joy to read!

SNOWWOWL.COM
The "Iroquois Legend of the Corn Husk Doll" was taken from this website. It is my understanding from reading the website that Snow Owl is deceased. My inquiry asking permission to use Snow Owl's story went unanswered. I appreciate Snow Owl's sharing this wonderful Native American legend, and I am proud to continue the story in the pages of this book.

JUSTIN GANNON
Justin is a young man at Richmond's Walmart who personally took me under his wing and made sure that the photographs taken at Bend School got developed ASAP even though none of the individual HP machines were in operation. Thank you!

RECOMMENDED APPALACHIAN BOOKS FOR CHILDREN

THE ADVENTURES OF MOLLY WHUPPIE
AND OTHER APPALACHIAN FOLKTALES
Anne Shelby

A IS FOR APPALACHIA! THE ALPHABET BOOK
OF APPALACHIAN HERITAGE
Linda Hager Pack

APPALACHIA: THE VOICES OF SLEEPING BIRDS
Cynthia Rylant

AN APPALACHIAN MOTHER GOOSE
James Still

APPALACHIAN SCRAPBOOK: AN A-B-C
OF GROWING UP IN THE MOUNTAINS
Pauline Cheek

ASHPET: AN APPALACHIAN TALE
Joanne Compton

A CERTAIN SMALL SHEPHERD
Rebecca Caudill

THE CHEROKEE
Emilie U. Lepthien

THE COFFIN QUILT
Ann Rinaldi
the feud between the Hatfields and the McCoys

COME A TIDE
George Ella Lyon

COME SING, JIMMY JO
Katherine Paterson

DID YOU CARRY THE FLAG TODAY, CHARLEY?
Rebecca Caudill

EIGHT HANDS ROUND:
A PATCHWORK ALPHABET
Ann Whitford Paul

FEARLESS JACK
Paul Brett Johnson

GENTLE'S HOLLER
Kerry Madden

GRANNY WILL YOUR DOG BITE
Gerald Milnes

IN COAL COUNTRY
Judith Hendershot

JACK OUTWITS THE GIANTS
Paul Brett Johnson

THE JACK TALES (AS TOLD BY RAY HICKS)
Lynn Salsi

JOURNEY CAKE, HO!
Ruth Sawyer

LITTLEJIM'S GIFT: AN APPALACHIAN
CHRISTMAS STORY
Gloria Houston

MAMA IS A MINER
George Ella Lyon

MARY ON HORSEBACK
Rosemary Wells

MISSING MAY
Cynthia Rylant

MOUNTAIN WEDDING
Faye Gibbons

MY GREAT-AUNT ARIZONA
Gloria Houston

OLD DRY FRYE: A DELICIOUSLY
FUNNY TALL TALE
Paul Brett Johnson

OLD SONGS & SINGING GAMES
collected and edited by Richard Chase

ONCE UPON A PONY:
A MOUNTAIN CHRISTMAS
Nancy Ward

ONE CHRISTMAS DAWN
Candice F. Ransom

THE PIG WHO WENT HOME ON SUNDAY
(AN APPALACHIAN FOLKTALE)
Donald Davis

PIONEER CHILDREN OF APPALACHIA
Joan Anderson

A POCKETFUL OF CRICKET
Rebecca Caudill
a Caldecott Honor book

POSSUM COME A-KNOCKIN'
Nancy Van Laan

RETURN TO BITTER CREEK
Doris Buchanan

SILVER PACKAGES:
AN APPALACHIAN CHRISTMAS STORY
Cynthia Rylant

SINGING GAMES AND PLAYPARTY GAMES
compiled by Richard Chase

SMOKY MOUNTAIN ROSE:
AN APPALACHIAN CINDERELLA
Alan Schroeder

SNOWBEAR WHITTINGTON:
AN APPALACHIAN BEAUTY AND THE BEAST
William H. Hooks

SODY SALLYRATUS
Teri Sloat

THE STORY OF THE CHEROKEE PEOPLE
Tom B. Underwood

THERE'S A HOLE IN MY BUCKET
William Stobbs

UP THE TRACKS TO GRANDMA'S
Judith Hendershot

WHEN UNCLE TOOK THE FIDDLE
Libba More Gray

WICKED JACK
adapted by Connie Nordhielm Woolridge

WILLIE PEARL
Michelle Y. Green

WILLIE PEARL UNDER THE MOUNTAIN
Michelle Y. Green

THE YEAR OF THE PERFECT CHRISTMAS TREE:
AN APPALACHIAN STORY
Gloria McLendon Houston

BIBLIOGRAPHY

Adcox, Susan. "Old-Fashioned Jump Rope Rhymes." About.Com Grandparents, http://grandparents.about.com. Retrieved June 20, 2010.

"Appalachian Toys." Compiled by J. R. Irwin. Museum of Appalachia, Norris, TN.

Avedon, Elliott. "Jackstraws, Pick-up-Sticks, Spellicans." Univ. of Waterloo Virtual Museum of Games, www.gamesmuseum.uwaterloo.ca/VirtualExhibits/Tablegames/. Retrieved August 7, 2010.

Bush, Florence Cope. *Dorie: Woman of the Mountains*. Knoxville, TN: Univ. of Tennessee Press, 1992.

Camp Silos. "The Story of Corn." Camp Silos, www.campsilos.org. Retrieved May 21, 2010.

Cheek, Angie, Lacy Hungr Nix, and Foxfire Students, eds. *The Foxfire 40th Anniversary Book: Faith, Family, and the Land*. New York: Anchor Books, 2006.

Eaton, Ercel Stidham. *Appalachian Yesterdays*. Fairfield, OH: Appalachian Yesterdays, 1982.

"Game of Graces." City of Tumwater, WA: Crafts and Games, www.ci.tumwater.wa.us/researchgameofgraces.htm. Retrieved April 15, 2010.

Grigg, B. "Anty Over the Shanty." Colebrook Historical Society, www.colebrookhistoricalsociety.org/Anty Over.htm. Retrieved July 14, 2010.

Mac Gregor, Megan. "Creation in the Hand: The Life in Folk Art Dolls." Historical Administration. American Toy Marble Museum, www.americantoymarbles.com/outdoor_handy_book_6.htm. Retrieved January 6, 2010.

Owl, Snow. "Iroquois Legend of the Corn Husk Doll." Snowwowl.com., http://snowwowl.com/naartcornhuskdolls.html#iroquois. Retrieved June 20, 2010.

Page, Linda Garland, and Hilton Smith, eds. *The Foxfire Book of Appalachian Toys and Games*. Chapel Hill: Univ. of North Carolina Press, 1993.

Schlosser, S. E. "Never Mind Them Watermelons." American Folklore, www.americanfolklore.net/folktales/a12.html. Retrieved January 6, 2010.

Slone, Verna Mae. *How We Talked*. Pippa Passes, KY: Pippa Valley, 1982.

Webb, Marian A. *Games for Younger Children*. New York: Wiliam Morrow, 1947.

Wigginton, Eliot, ed. *Foxfire 6 Shoemaking, Gourd Banjos and Songbows, One Hundred Toys and Games, Wooden Locks, a Water-Powered Sawmill, and Other Affairs of Just Plain Living*. Garden City, NY: Anchor Press/Doubleday, 1980.

ABOUT THE AUTHOR AND THE ILLUSTRATOR

LINDA HAGER PACK

Linda Hager Pack currently lives in Richmond, Kentucky, but she grew up in the small town of Hamlin, West Virginia, where she was reared by her parents, aunts, uncles, and grandparents to be a proper mountain young'un. She earned a Bachelor of Science in Education and a Master of Arts in Education from Eastern Kentucky University. Linda taught elementary school for twenty-two years in West Virginia and Kentucky, and she was presented the Ashland Oil Teacher Award by Kentucky governor Paul Patton in 1996. After retiring from teaching elementary education, Linda enjoyed teaching children's literature at Eastern Kentucky University. She has always taken pleasure in following the advice she often gave her students: Write about what you know and what you love. For Linda that has meant writing about Appalachia, the place she loves best, and its people. The proof is in her first book, *A is for Appalachia! The Alphabet Book of Appalachian Heritage.*

PAT BANKS

Pat works primarily in watercolor. Her fascination with the medium, combined with her studies and travels, has given her a unique lens to interpret the world, especially eastern Kentucky, her home. The beauty of the hills, valleys, and rivers inspires the expression of an artist and the concern of an environmentalist. By taking the time to walk paths in the woods and fields, float down the eternal streams, and study the "wild things," she has come to realize how fragile and precious this wondrous place is. Pat brings the spontaneity and freshness of the watercolor medium to the challenge and intensity of her subjects. Her work is shown and sold in dozens of galleries and venues throughout the region and has been displayed in shows at the Evansville Museum, the Kentucky Museum of Art and Craft, the Owensboro Museum, and other museums. She lives and works in northern Madison County in the home and studio she and her husband, Alan, built. They grow gardens, float on the Kentucky River, and look for the occasional adventure.

THE END

Thank you for exploring the pages of this book to learn about the toys and games that Appalachia's children enjoyed.
Books make good friends. Thank you for becoming friends with this one. As we say in Appalachia, "Don't be a stranger."